ANDREW LLOYD WEBBER™

DIVAS

HAL•LEONARD® CORPORATION

7777 W. BLUEMOUND RD. P.O. BOX 13819 MILWAUKEE, WI 53213

ANDREW LLOYD WEBBER™

DIVAS

ISBN-13: 978-1-4234-2576-2
ISBN-10: 1-4234-2576-6

Visit Hal Leonard Online at
www.halleonard.com

ALL I ASK OF YOU

FROM 'THE PHANTOM OF THE OPERA'

Music by Andrew Lloyd Webber
Lyrics by Charles Hart
Additional Lyrics by Richard Stilgoe

Andante

No more talk of dark-ness, for-

-get these wide-eyed fears; I'm here, no-thing can harm you, my words will warm and calm you.

Let me be your free-dom, let day-light dry your tears; I'm

Love me, that's all I ask of you.

A-ny-where you go, let me go too; love me that's all I ask of you.

ANOTHER SUITCASE IN ANOTHER HALL

FROM 'EVITA'

Words by Tim Rice
Music by Andrew Lloyd Webber

Be - ing used to trou - ble I an - ti - - - ci - pate it but
ev - ery time it mat - ters all my words de - sert me so
won't re - call the names and plac - es of this sad oc - ca - sion, but

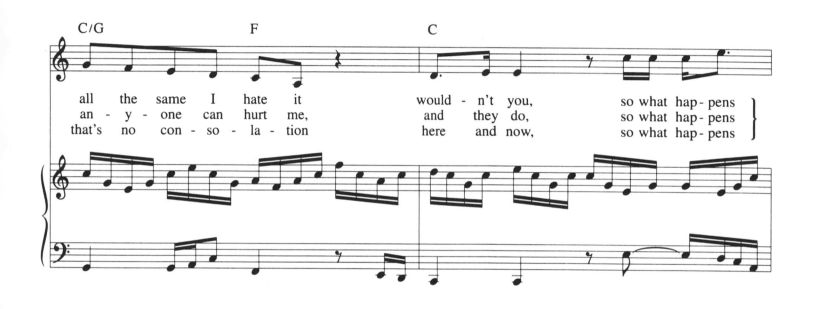

all the same I hate it would - n't you, so what hap - pens
an - y - one can hurt me, and they do, so what hap - pens
that's no con - so - la - tion here and now, so what hap - pens

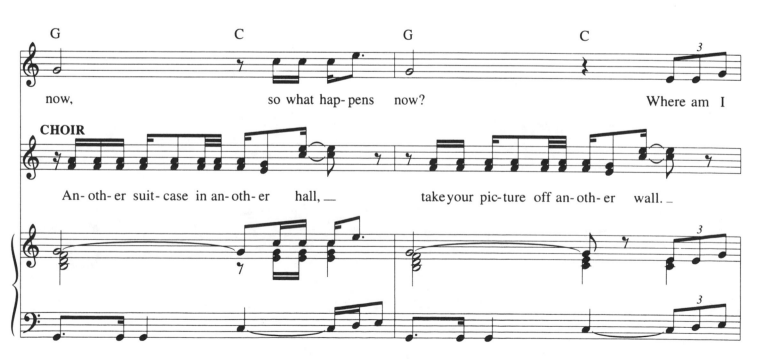

now, so what hap - pens now? Where am I

CHOIR

An - oth - er suit - case in an - oth - er hall, __ take your pic - ture off an - oth - er wall. __

BUENOS AIRES

FROM 'EVITA'

Words by Tim Rice
Music by Andrew Lloyd Webber

in at your flood, give me speed, give me lights, set me hum-ming. Shoot me

up with your blood, wine me up with your nights, watch me com-ing.

All___ I want___ is a whole lot of ex-cess.___

Tell the sing-er this is where I'm play-ing.

Stand back Bue-nos Air - es be - cause you ought-a know what-cha gon-na get in me,___ just a lit - tle bit of star qual-i-ty,___ And_____ if ev - er I go too far,___ it's be-cause of the

(drum fill)

19

Dialogue

You're a   tramp, you're a treat, you will shine to the death, you are

shod - dy But your flesh, you are meat, you shall have ev-'ry breath in my bo - dy

Put___ me down___ for a life - time of suc - cess.___

Give me cre - dit, I'll find ways of pay - ing.

Ri - o de - la Pla - ta. Flo - ri - da Cor - ri - en - tes!

Nu-ev-e de Jul - i - o,___ all___ I want to___ know.___

Stand back! Buen-os Air-es! Be-cause you ought-a know

what-cha gon-na get in me___ just a lit-tle touch of, just___ a lit-

-tle touch of, just___ a lit-tle touch of star qua-li-ty.___

AS IF WE NEVER SAID GOODBYE

FROM 'SUNSET BOULEVARD'

Music by Andrew Lloyd Webber

Lyrics by Don Black & Christopher Hampton,
with contributions by Amy Powers

Moderato

colla voce

I don't know why I'm fright-ened___ I know my way a-round here.___ The

card-board trees, the paint-ed seas,___ the sound here._____ Yes, a

world to re-dis-cov - er,_____ but I'm not in a-ny hur - ry,_____ and I

need a mo - ment. The whis-pered con-ver-sa - tions_____ in

So watch me fly,__ we all know I__ can do it._____ Could I

stop my hand from shak - ing?____ Has there ev - er been a mo - ment____ with so

much to live for? The whis-pered con - ver - sa - tions____ in

ov - er-crowd-ed hall - ways,____ so much to say, not just to - day,__ but

28

DON'T CRY FOR ME ARGENTINA

FROM 'EVITA'

Words by Tim Rice
Music by Andrew Lloyd Webber

nines at six - es and se - vens with you.

2. I had to let it hap - pen, I had to change; could-n't stay all my life down at

heel, look-ing out of the win-dow, stay-ing out of the sun. So I chose

free - dom, run-ning a-round try-ing ev-ry-thing new; but no-thing im-pressed me at

look at me to know that ev - 'ry word is true.

Refrain grandioso
Orchestra tutti

I DON'T KNOW HOW TO LOVE HIM

FROM 'JESUS CHRIST SUPERSTAR'

Words by Tim Rice
Music by Andrew Lloyd Webber

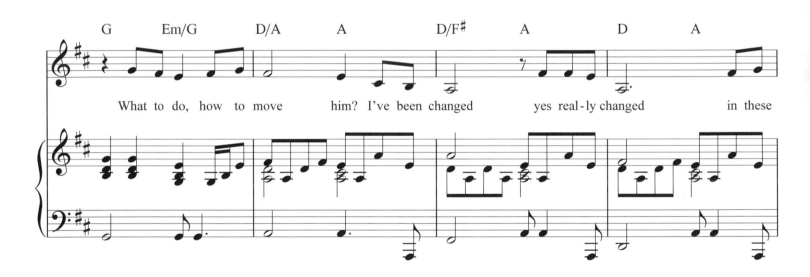

LEARN TO BE LONELY

FROM 'THE PHANTOM OF THE OPERA'

Music by Andrew Lloyd Webber
Lyrics by Charles Hart

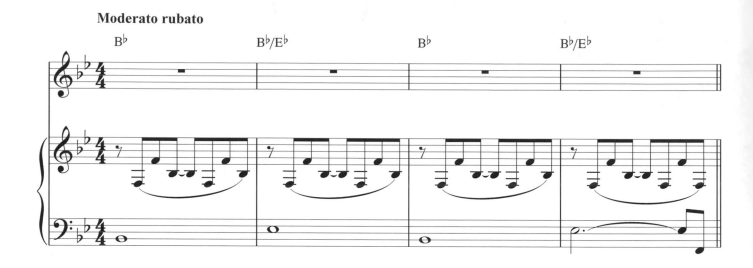

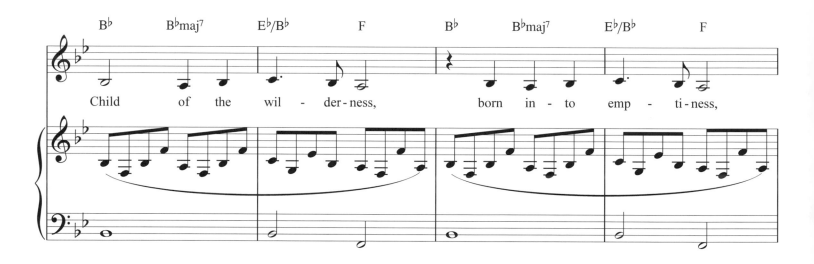

LOVE CHANGES EVERYTHING
FROM 'ASPECTS OF LOVE'

Music by Andrew Lloyd Webber
Lyrics by Don Black and Charles Hart

1. Love, love chan - ges ev - 'ry - thing: hands and fa - ces, earth and sky.

2. Love, love chan - ges ev - 'ry - thing: days are long - er, words mean more.

Love, love chan - ges ev - 'ry - thing: how you

Love, can break the strong - est heart, pain is

poco rit.   **a tempo**

years.   Love_____ bursts in and sud- den- ly,   all our

wis - dom   dis - ap - pears.   Love_____ makes fools of

ev - ’ry- one: all the rules   we make   are bro - ken.   Yes

love,_____   love chan- ges   ev - ’ry- thing.   Live or per - ish   in its

MEMORY

FROM 'CATS'

Music by Andrew Lloyd Webber

Text by Trevor Nunn after T.S. Eliot

Day - light.___ I must wait for the sun - rise,___ I must think of a new life___ and I must-n't give in._____ When the dawn comes to-night will be a me-mo-ry too___ and a new day_____ will be - gin.

Burnt out ends of smo - ky days,—— the stale cold smell—— of morn - ing.—— The street lamp dies, an - oth - er night is ov - er,—— an - oth - er day is dawn - ing.——

Touch me.____ It's so ea-sy to leave me____ all a-lone with the me-mory____ of my days in the sun.____ If you touch me you'll un-der-stand what hap-pi-ness is. Look a new day has be-gun.

THE MUSIC OF THE NIGHT

FROM 'THE PHANTOM OF THE OPERA'

Music by Andrew Lloyd Webber

Lyrics by Charles Hart

Additional Lyrics by Richard Stilgoe

night. Let your mind start a jour-ney through a strange, new world; leave all

thoughts of the world you knew be - fore. Let your soul take you where you long to

be! On - ly then can you be - long to me.

Float -ing, fall - ing, sweet in-tox - i - ca - tion. Touch me, trust me, sa-vour each sen-sa - tion.

Let the dream be-gin, let your dark-er side give in to the pow-er of the mu-sic that I write, the

pow-er of the mu-sic of the night.

You a-lone can make my song take

flight, help me make the mu-sic of the night.

THE PERFECT YEAR

FROM 'SUNSET BOULEVARD'

Music by Andrew Lloyd Webber
Lyrics by Don Black and Christopher Hampton

1. Ring out the old,____ bring in the new,____ a mid-night wish____ to share with
hear____ the mus-ic play,____ your eyes say all____ there is to

you.____ Your lips are warm,____ my head is light,____ were we in love____ be-fore to-
say.____ The stars can fade,____ and they can shine,____ long as your face____ is next to

SURRENDER

FROM 'SUNSET BOULEVARD'

Music by Andrew Lloyd Webber
Lyrics by Don Black and Christopher Hampton

Simply, like a lullaby

NORMA: No more wars to fight, white flags fly to-night,

you are out of dan - ger now.

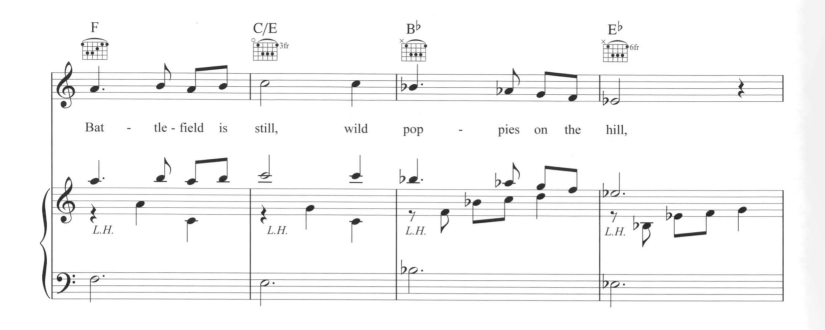

Bat - tle - field is still, wild pop - pies on the hill,

peace can on - ly come when you sur - ren - der.

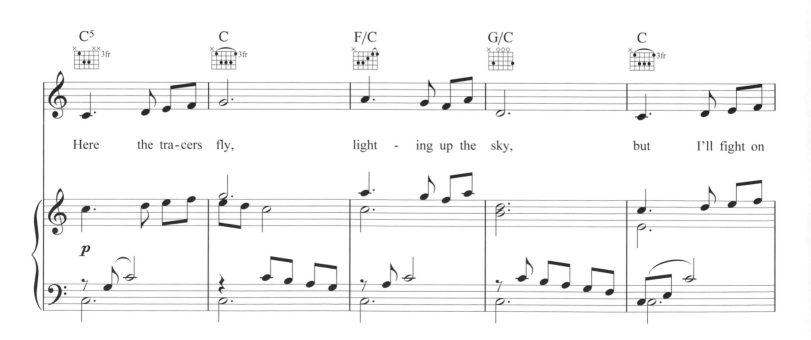

Here the tra - cers fly, light - ing up the sky, but I'll fight on

RAINBOW HIGH

FROM 'EVITA'

Words by Tim Rice
Music by Andrew Lloyd Webber

I'm not a se-con rate Queen get-ting kicks with a crown!

Next stop will be Eu-rope! The

Rain - bow's gon - na tour,_____ dressed up, some - where to

L'istesso tempo

Più mosso - Allegro moderato

go; we'll put on a show!_____

Look out might - y Eu - rope! Be - cause you ough - ta know what cha gon - na get in me:___ Just a lit - tle touch of, just___ a lit - tle touch of Ar - gen - ti - na's brand of star qual - i - ty!___

73

TAKE THAT LOOK OFF YOUR FACE

FROM 'SONG AND DANCE'

Music by Andrew Lloyd Webber

Lyrics by Don Black

76

TIRE TRACKS AND BROKEN HEARTS

FROM 'WHISTLE DOWN THE WIND'

Music by Andrew Lloyd Webber
Lyrics by Jim Steinman

fine per - fume,_____ a pow - der blue Cor - vette.____ If there's a
(3.) push - up bra,_____ I want some sa - tin___ sheets.____ Give me some

slow - er death_ than liv - ing here and now,_ they have - n't found it yet._____ I need a
real rich_ food;_____ I want some suc - cu - lent sweets._____ I want you

man who knows_____ what I am real - ly___ worth.____ And I
by my side,_____ you'll be all my___ own.____ I don't

don't give a damn_ a - bout life af - ter death,_ but I got - ta get some proof that there's a
know what I want_ half the time, but I know_ that I don't wan - na spend an - oth - er

WHISTLE DOWN THE WIND

FROM 'WHISTLE DOWN THE WIND'

Music by Andrew Lloyd Webber

Lyrics by Jim Steinman

I'll be there to hold you, I'll be there to stop the chills and all the weep- ing.___ Make it

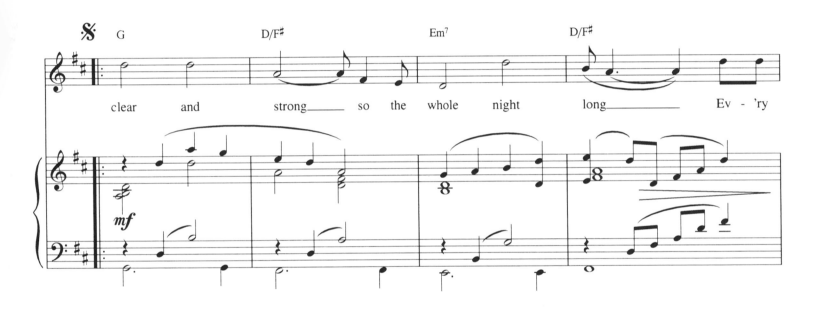

clear and strong___ so the whole night long___ Ev - 'ry

sig - nal that you send, un - til the ve - ry end I will not a - ban - don you my pre-cious friend, so

try and stem the tide_____ then you'll raise a ban - ner____ send a

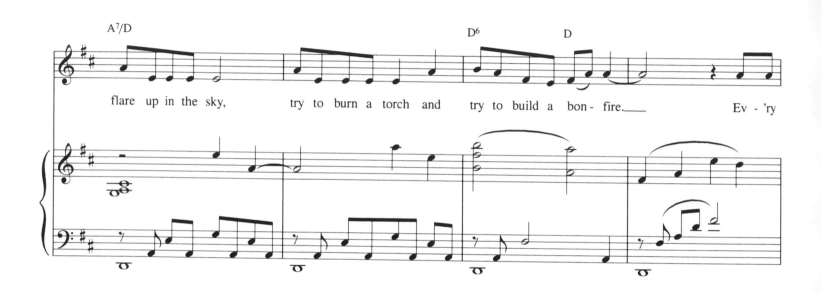

flare up in the sky, try to burn a torch and try to build a bon - fire.____ Ev - 'ry

sig - nal that you send, un - til the ve - ry end I'm there.____ So

whis-tle down the wind for I have al-ways been right here.

Make it

whis-tle down the wind for I have al-ways been right there.

WITH ONE LOOK

FROM 'SUNSET BOULEVARD'

Music by Andrew Lloyd Webber

Lyrics by Don Black & Christopher Hampton,

with contributions by Amy Powers

Lento moderato

mp espressivo

With one look I can break your heart, with one look I play ev - ery part.

I can make your sad heart sing. With one look you'll know all you need to know.

With one smile I'm the girl next door or the love that you've hun - gered for.

Si - lent mu-sic starts to play. One tear in my eye makes the whole world cry.

With one look they'll for-give the past, they'll re - joice I've re-turned at last

to my peo-ple in the dark, still out there in the dark.

TELL ME ON A SUNDAY

FROM 'SONG AND DANCE'

Music by Andrew Lloyd Webber
Lyrics by Don Black

cov-ered with trees.___ Tell me on a Sun - day please.
got chim-pan - zees. ___ Tell me on a Sun - day

please.   Don't want to know___ who's to blame___
Inst.

it won't help know-ing.   Don't want to fight day and night
I don't want to fight day and night

bad e - nough ___ you're go - ing.___ } Don't leave in sil - ence
bad e - nough ___ you're go - ing.___ }